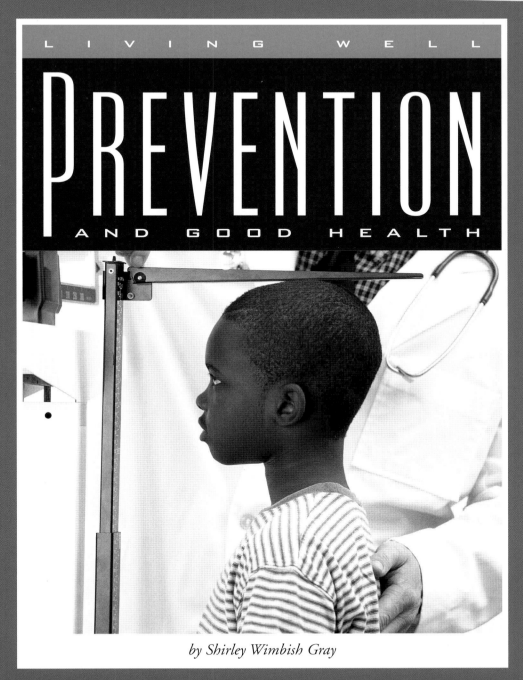

# LIVING WELL

# PREVENTION

## AND GOOD HEALTH

*by Shirley Wimbish Gray*

THE CHILD'S WORLD®

CHANHASSEN, MINNESOTA

**The Child's World**

Published in the United States of America by The Child's World®
P.O. Box 326, Chanhassen, MN 55317-0326
800-599-READ
www.childsworld.com

*Subject adviser:*
*Diana Ruschhaupt,*
*Director of Programs,*
*Ruth Lilly Health*
*Education Center,*
*Indianapolis,*
*Indianapolis*

Photo Credits: Cover: Creatas; Bettmann/Corbis: 7, 17, 18, 21; Corbis: 9 (Ronnie Kaufman), 10, 12 (Ed Bock), 14 (Lester V. Bergman), 15 (Joseph Sohm; ChromoSohm Inc.), 19, 21 right (Reuters New Media Inc.), 23 (Charles Krebs), 27 (Chris Rogers), 31 (Jose Luis Pelaez, Inc.); Custom Medical Stock Photo: 6, 8 16, 20, 24, 26; David Young-Wolff/PhotoEdit: 22, 25; Michael Newman/PhotoEdit: 13, 25 right; Photo Edit: 5 (Tony Freeman), 11 (Patrick Olear), 11 right (Dennis MacDonald), 15 right (A. Ramey), 29 (Richard Hutchings).

The Child's World®: Mary Berendes, Publishing Director

Editorial Directions, Inc.: E. Russell Primm, Editorial Director; Elizabeth K. Martin, Line Editor; Katie Marsico, Assistant Editor; Olivia Nellums, Editorial Assistant; Susan Hindman, Copy Editor; Sarah E. De Capua, Proofreader; Peter Garnham and Chris Simms, Fact Checkers; Tim Griffin/IndexServ, Indexer; Elizabeth K. Martin and Matthew Messbarger, Photo Researchers and Selectors

**Library of Congress Cataloging-in-Publication Data**
Gray, Shirley W.
  Prevention and good health / by Shirley Wimbish Gray.
      p. cm. — (Living well)
Includes index.
Summary: Explains the importance of cleanliness and other preventive measures to
maintain a healthy body.
  ISBN 1-59296-083-9 (lib. bdg. : alk. paper)
 1. Health—Juvenile literature. 2. Medicine, Preventive—Juvenile literature. 3.
Vaccination—Juvenile literature. [1. Health. 2. Medicine, Preventive. 3. Vaccination.] I.
Title. II. Series: Living well (Child's World (Firm)
  RA777.G674 2004
  613—dc21                                             2003006281

# TABLE OF CONTENTS

# CHAPTER ONE

# MAKE SURE
# YOU STAY HEALTHY!

Todd slowly walked to the car. He was not happy. His mother was

taking him to the doctor's office to get a shot. She said he needed a

vaccination (vak-suh-NAY-shun) before the new school year started.

"I don't know why I have to get a shot," he said as he got in the

car. "I'm never sick, and I never miss any school."

"That's because we do things to prevent you from getting sick,"

his mother answered.

At the doctor's office, the nurse explained what she was going

to do. Todd looked away as she stuck the needle in his arm. It hurt

for a second and then it burned. Just as he opened his mouth to

complain, the burning stopped.

"That's it," the nurse said as she put a bandage on his arm.

"Your arm might be sore and feel hot for the next couple of days. That's normal."

Todd was surprised at how quickly it was over. "Come on, Mom," he said as he walked quickly back to the car. "I feel fine. I want to go home and ride my bike."

Most children are like Todd. They do not want to get a shot. But they also do not want to get sick. They would miss out on doing things they enjoy. They could not ride their bikes or play with friends. Shots help you keep doing the things you love. There are lots of other things you can do to make sure you stay healthy, too.

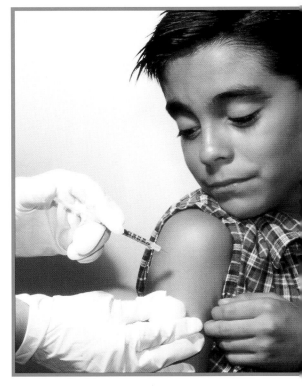

*Getting a shot wasn't as bad as Todd had feared. He barely even noticed.*

# CHAPTER TWO

# HOW DOES YOUR
# BODY FIGHT DISEASE?

Your body has an important weapon that helps it prevent disease—

the immune (im-MYOON) system. It includes white blood cells that

float throughout the body in the blood. If a germ invades the body, the white blood cells attack. Often, the white blood cells can get rid of a germ without you ever feeling sick.

Scientists have learned ways to help boost the immune system. One way is

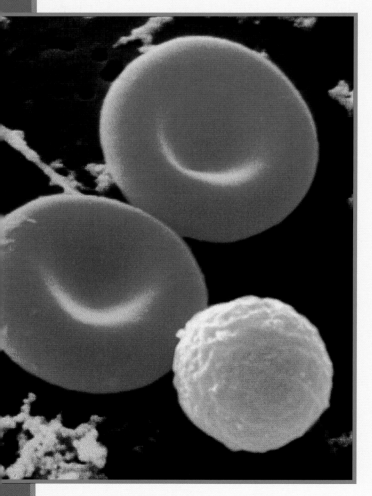

*White blood cells (lower right) such*
*as the one shown here help your body fight diseases.*

to give the body a **vaccine.** Have you ever heard of the mumps? What about the measles (MEE-zulz)? These are two diseases that once made children very sick. Today,

*Thanks to vaccines, you will probably never get mumps. Years ago, however, it was a common disease for American children to get.*

vaccines prevent most children from getting diseases like these.

Once in the body, a vaccine helps the immune system build **antibodies.** They help the body fight a disease. Children in the United States get vaccines for about 10 different diseases before they start school. Most children get vaccines through shots in their arms or legs.

Not all vaccines are given through shots, though. Doctors are testing new ways to get them into the body. One idea is to use a nose spray. This has been tested with the flu vaccine. Most children and adults think it would be better than getting a flu shot every year!

What you eat and how much you eat also helps your body stay healthy. The body uses **nutrients** (noo-TREE-ents) from food as building blocks. For example, calcium

*Eating well and getting your shots can help prevent this virus, the flu, from making you sick.*

(KAL-see-um) is a nutrient found mainly in milk and other dairy foods. The body uses calcium to build bones and teeth. Children need at

*Drinking milk can help you prevent osteoporosis.*

least four servings of calcium every day.

Adults who do not have enough calcium can develop osteoporosis (oss-tee-oh-puh-RO-sis). If this happens, their bones become weak and can break easily.

**Vitamins** are also nutrients. Vitamin C is an important nutrient found in foods. It helps make the immune system

*Vitamin C helps build your immune system.*
*Drinking orange juice is one healthy way to get the Vitamin C that you need.*

stronger. That helps your body prevent infections, like colds and

the flu.

Vitamin C is found in fruit like oranges, grapefruits, and

strawberries. You should eat some of these every day. Some people

take a vitamin tablet to make sure they are getting enough.

# CHAPTER THREE

# WHAT ABOUT CHECKUPS?

It might seem weird to go to the doctor when you are healthy, but that is the best time to go. You should make regular visits to the doctor and dentist for checkups. They can let you know if your body is in good shape. They will also let you and your family know if your body

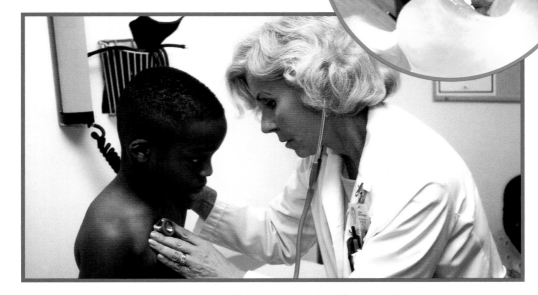

*Regular checkups will help you stay healthy. Your doctor and dentist can often catch any health problems before they really start.*

*Glasses help your eyes work better. They make it easier to see the world around you!*

needs some help. Getting help when you are young may prevent

bigger problems when you are older.

Sometimes as the body grows, the different parts of the eye will

not work together as they should. If that happens, you may not be able

to read the blackboard in class. Have your eyes checked to make sure

everything is working. This is easy and does not hurt. First, you are

asked to cover one eye and read letters off a chart. Then the other eye

is covered and you read again. Children who have trouble reading the

charts may need eyeglasses or contact lenses.

Have you ever had your hearing tested? Sometimes, the school nurse will do this with everyone in your class. The nurse will use a machine that makes different types of sounds. You will listen for the sounds through a set of earphones. Some of the sounds will be easy to hear. Others will be hard. If you hear the sound, you will be asked to raise your hand.

*A simple hearing test can make a big difference.*
*A doctor can tell if hearing aids might help you.*

## Stand Up Straight!

One of the easiest health checkups helps make sure that you can stand straight and tall. It's called a scoliosis (sko-lee-OH-sis) test. For this test, you will be asked to bend over and touch your toes. Then a nurse or a parent will run a finger down your spine to see if it is curved.

Children with scoliosis have S-shaped or C-shaped curves on their spines. If the curve is mild, no treatment is needed. As a child grows, the curve might get worse. If this happens, then a back brace or surgery might be needed.

Regular trips to the dentist are also important. Children need to go two times a year to make sure they do not have any **cavities**. Dentists will also check to make sure that the teeth are growing the right way. If not, a child may need to wear braces. This can prevent more serious teeth problems as an adult.

# CHAPTER FOUR

# HOW DO DOCTORS PREVENT DISEASES?

**T**oday, the average adult in the United States

will live to be about 75 years old. Two

hundred years ago, the average adult

was lucky to live to age 45. Why

do people enjoy longer lives today?

*Americans live much longer now than they did years ago.*
*Today, seniors stay healthy through many different activities.*

*Doctor Edward Jenner*
*discovered a way to prevent smallpox.*

It is because we have learned how to prevent many diseases.

For thousands of years, smallpox was a deadly disease. People who got this virus were sick with high fevers and had a rash that covered their bodies. Thousands of people died each year from smallpox.

Even today, there is no cure for smallpox. But doctors know how to prevent it. A family doctor named Edward Jenner did an experiment in 1796 that helped the world get rid of smallpox. His work helped doctors learn how to prevent other diseases, too.

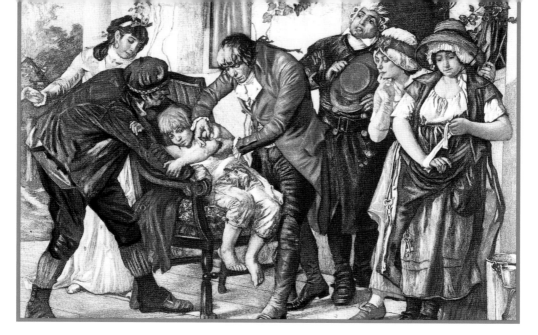

*Dr. Jenner's experiment seemed scary, but it worked.*
*Young James Phipps did not get smallpox.*

Dr. Jenner noticed that young women who milked cows often got a minor skin rash called cowpox. They caught it from the cows. But if they had cowpox, they did not catch smallpox. Dr. Jenner thought maybe cowpox could help prevent smallpox.

He needed to test his idea. An eight-year-old boy named James Phipps agreed to help. Dr. Jenner scratched James's arm with a little bit of fluid from a cowpox rash. Six weeks later he scratched James's arm with smallpox. James did not get sick.

Some people thought Dr. Jenner's idea was scary and would not try it. Others knew that smallpox had to be prevented. As Dr. Jenner increased his testing, more people were able to avoid getting smallpox. Soon, a vaccination against smallpox was created. Vaccination comes from the Latin word *vacca*. It means "cow" and helps us remember what Dr. Jenner did.

The smallpox vaccine was used around the world. Fewer and fewer people died from the disease. In the 1970s, doctors announced that smallpox had been wiped out from

*Over time, worldwide smallpox vaccinations helped to get rid of the disease completely.*

the face of the Earth. No cases of smallpox have been reported in almost 30 years.

Today, scientists hope to get rid of polio, too. No cases of polio have been reported in the United States since 1994. But it is still found in other countries. Doctors hope that this disease will not exist in any country by 2005.

## Eating Sugar to Stay Healthy

For many years, polio was a dangerous disease. It passed easily from one person to another. As a result, thousands and thousands of children developed it. Many of them were unable to walk after they recovered from the disease. Even U.S. president Franklin Roosevelt suffered from polio.

In 1957, Albert Sabin tested a new vaccine to prevent polio. This vaccine had to be swallowed, so doctors decided to put drops of it on cubes of sugar. To be fully protected, a person had to eat one sugar cube a week for three weeks.

The new vaccine worked. In 1960, there were more than 2,000 cases of polio. By 1965, only 61 cases were reported. Eating sugar cubes that contained the vaccine helped prevent a bad disease.

# CHAPTER FIVE

# HOW CAN YOU KEEP
# GERMS FROM SPREADING?

**V**accinations are not the only way to prevent bad diseases. Today,

we know how to prevent many germs from growing or spreading.

That prevents people from getting sick because it keeps them from

coming into contact with germs.

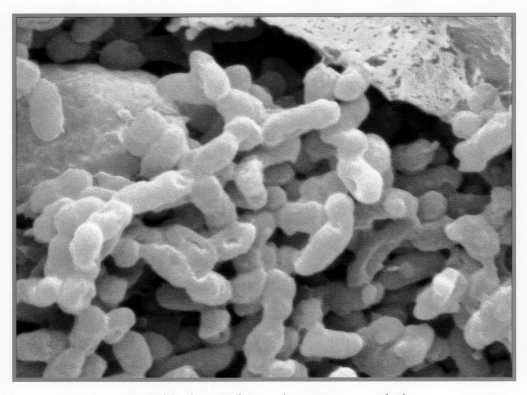

*Germs like these can be anywhere, even in your food.*
*Learn how to keep germs from spreading so that you can stay healthy.*

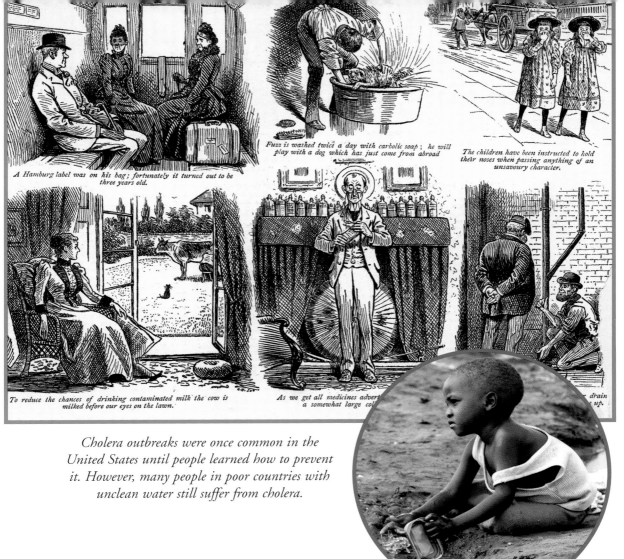

*A Hamburg label was on his bag; fortunately it turned out to be three years old.*

*Fuzz is washed twice a day with carbolic soap; he will play with a dog which has just come from abroad*

*The children have been instructed to hold their noses when passing anything of an unsavoury character.*

*To reduce the chances of drinking contaminated milk the cow is milked before our eyes on the lawn.*

*As we get all medicines advert[...] a somewhat large col[...]*

[...] drain [...] up.

*Cholera outbreaks were once common in the United States until people learned how to prevent it. However, many people in poor countries with unclean water still suffer from cholera.*

Cholera (KOLL-er-ah) is a disease that used to kill thousands of people in the United States. It comes from a germ that can live in water. People got sick after drinking bad water. Now we treat our drinking water so it does not have germs in it.

*Drinking bottled water while hiking or camping will help you steer clear of germs.*

Remember never to drink water from a lake or pond. It is also not safe to drink from a river or stream. The water might have cholera or other germs in it. Always carry fresh drinking water when you go hiking or camping.

Mosquitoes often carry diseases that make humans sick. Starting

in 2001, some people in the United States began catching a rare

disease called West Nile virus. They got this disease from mosquitoes.

Cities and states often spray chemicals in areas where mosquitoes

live. You can help get rid of mosquitoes, too. These little insects lay

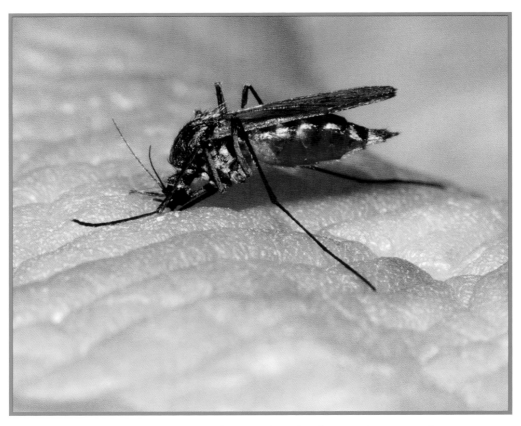

*Mosquitoes often spread diseases when they bite people or animals.*

their eggs in small pools of water. Check your yard regularly in the summer. Turn over pots, pails, or bowls that might collect water. Then mosquitoes will not want to lay eggs in your yard.

*Mosquitoes like to lay their eggs in water.*
*Getting rid of water in your yard will help keep mosquitoes away.*

*Covering your mouth and washing
your hands are two simple things
you can do to stop germs from spreading.*

Germs that cause colds and

the flu travel easily in the air. Each

time a sick person coughs or sneezes, thousands

of germs fly into the air. What can you do to keep from getting sick?

Cover your mouth when you cough or sneeze. Then wash your hands.

Washing with soap and water is the best way to get rid of germs.

Germs can also live in raw meat such as chicken or fish. If the meat is not cooked well enough, people can get the germs when they eat the meat. Make sure you eat meat that is well-done and not red. Also, be sure to wash knives and anything else in the kitchen that come in contact with raw meat.

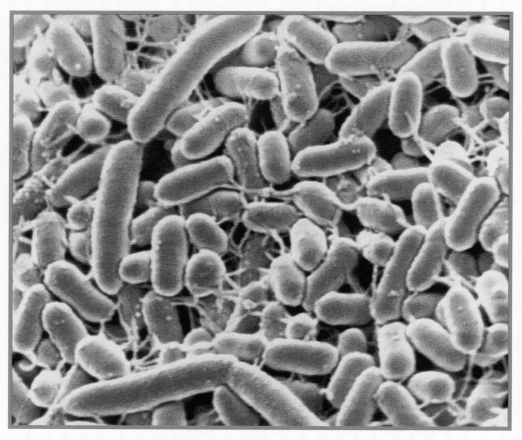

*These salmonella germs live in raw chicken meat or in raw eggs.*
*Cooking the meat and eggs long enough will keep the germs from making you sick.*

*There are plenty of things you can do to prevent disease every day.*

Fighting disease is everyone's job. What have you done to fight disease today?

# Glossary

**antibodies** (AN-tee-bod-eez) Antibodies are proteins the body makes in reaction to germs and other foreign matter that enters the body.

**cavities** (KAV-uh-teez) Cavities are pitted areas in teeth caused by bacteria and decay.

**nutrients** (NOO-tree-uhnts) Nutrients found in foods are needed to live and stay healthy.

**vaccine** (vak-SEEN) A vaccine is something given to the body to help it build an immunity or resist a disease.

**vitamins** (VYE-tuh-minz) Vitamins are made by living things. The body gets vitamins from food and needs them to work properly.

# Questions and Answers about Prevention

**Could smallpox come back again?** Maybe. Some people think that smallpox could be used as a weapon. If so, doctors know what to do. There are plenty of smallpox vaccines to help keep people from getting sick.

**How long do I need to wash my hands?** You should rub your hands together with soap and water for about 10 to 15 seconds. Then rinse your hands and dry them on a clean towel. The combination of the soap and the scrubbing action gets rid of the germs.

**Does everyone need to get a flu shot?** Doctors tell us that older adults, such as your grandparents, should get a flu shot every year. Children with asthma and other types of diseases should also get one. If you are generally healthy, then you and your parents can decide if you need the vaccination.

# Did You Know?

▶ The kitchen and the bathroom have more germs than any other rooms in the house. Cleaning surfaces in these rooms every day with a disinfectant will help keep your family healthy.

▶ Girls are more likely to have scoliosis than boys.

▶ Yellow fever is a virus that is spread by mosquitoes. In the 1800s, thousands of people in the United States died from large outbreaks of the virus. Today, yellow fever is common only in Africa.

▶ In 2002, 275 people in the United States died from the West Nile virus.

*Keep your bathroom and kitchen free of germs.*

# How to Learn More about Prevention

### At the Library: Fiction
Anderson, Laurie Halse. *Fever, 1793.*
New York: Simon & Schuster Books for Young Readers, 2000.

Kimmel, Elizabeth Cody, and Nora Koerber (illustrator). *Balto and the Great Race.*
New York: Random House, 1999.

### At the Library: Nonfiction
Kehret, Peg, and Denise Shanahan. *Small Steps: The Year I Got Polio.*
Morton Grove, Ill.: Albert Whitman, 1996.

McGinty, Alice B. *Staying Healthy: Dental Care.*
New York: PowerKids Press, 1997.

Silverstein, Alvin, Virginia Silverstein, and Laura Silverstein Nunn. *What Are Germs?*
Danbury, Conn.: Franklin Watts, Inc., 2002.

### On the Web
Visit our home page for lots of links about good health:
*http://www.childsworld.com/links.html*

Note to Parents, Teachers, and Librarians: We routinely verify our
Web links to make sure they're safe, active sites—so encourage your
readers to check them out!

### Through the Mail or by Phone
Centers for Disease Control and Prevention
1600 Clifton Road
MS C-04
Atlanta, GA 30333
404/639-3311

**National Institute of Allergy and Infectious Diseases**
Building 31, Room 7A-50
31 Center Drive MSC 2520
Bethesda, MD 20892-2520

*Regular trips to the doctor will help prevent diseases and keep you healthy as you grow.*

# Index

## About the Author

**Shirley Wimbish Gray** has been a writer and educator for more than 25 years and has published more than a dozen nonfiction books for children. She also coordinates cancer education programs at the University of Arkansas for Medical Sciences and consults as a writer with scientists and physicians. She lives with her husband and two sons in Little Rock, Arkansas.